Neighborhood Safari

Finches

by Dalton Rains

www.focusreaders.com

Copyright © 2025 by Focus Readers®, Mendota Heights, MN 55120. All rights reserved. No part of this book may be reproduced or utilized in any form or by any means without written permission from the publisher.

Focus Readers is distributed by North Star Editions:
sales@northstareditions.com | 888-417-0195

Produced for Focus Readers by Red Line Editorial.

Photographs ©: Shutterstock Images, cover, 1, 4, 6, 8, 10, 12, 14, 17, 18, 21

Library of Congress Cataloging-in-Publication Data
Names: Rains, Dalton, author.
Title: Finches / by Dalton Rains.
Description: Mendota Heights, MN: Focus Readers, [2025] | Series: Neighborhood safari | Includes bibliographical references and index. | Audience: Grades K-1
Identifiers: LCCN 2023059772 (print) | LCCN 2023059773 (ebook) | ISBN 9798889981756 (hardcover) | ISBN 9798889982319 (paperback) | ISBN 9798889983422 (pdf) | ISBN 9798889982876 (ebook)
Subjects: LCSH: Finches--Juvenile literature.
Classification: LCC QL696.P246 R35 2025 (print) | LCC QL696.P246 (ebook) | DDC 598.8/8--dc23/eng/20240123
LC record available at https://lccn.loc.gov/2023059772
LC ebook record available at https://lccn.loc.gov/2023059773

Printed in the United States of America
Mankato, MN
082024

About the Author

Dalton Rains is a writer and editor from Minnesota.

Table of Contents

CHAPTER 1
Finding Food 5

CHAPTER 2
Body Parts 9

CHAPTER 3
Feathers and Beaks 13

THAT'S AMAZING!
Spreading Seeds 16

CHAPTER 4
A Finch's Life 19

Focus on Finches • 22
Glossary • 23
To Learn More • 24
Index • 24

Chapter 1

Finding Food

A bright finch flies through a field. It dives toward a flower. The finch scoops up seeds with its beak. It chews up the seeds. Then it flies back to its nest.

Finches live in many places. Some nest in trees. Some nest on rock **ledges**. Others live on buildings. Finches make nests with different objects. They may use sticks or feathers.

Fun Fact

Sometimes finches use nests left behind by other birds.

Chapter 2

Body Parts

Finches are small birds. They have feathers all over their bodies. Finches use their eyes to spot things. They use their beaks to pick up food.

Finches have two feet. Each foot has three toes that face forward. One toe faces backward. That way, finches can grip branches and other **perches**.

Fun Fact Tail feathers help finches balance when they fly.

Chapter 3

Feathers and Beaks

Finches come in many different colors. The food a finch eats can change the color of its feathers. Females often **mate** with brightly colored males.

Finches also have different beak shapes. Some beaks are narrow and sharp. These are good for picking up **insects**. Others are long. They can reach inside **cacti**.

Fun Fact

Some finches live in **grasslands**. Their feathers usually have dull colors. They **blend** in with the brown ground.

That's Amazing!

Spreading Seeds

Finches help spread seeds to new places. The birds may knock down seeds from plants. Or they may spread seeds farther away. That happens when finches eat seeds. The seeds end up in their poop. Then those seeds grow in new places.

Chapter 4

A Finch's Life

Finches mate during the winter. Females lay eggs in the spring and summer. Babies hatch after about two weeks. At first, they cannot fly.

Both parents help feed the babies. After two or three weeks, the chicks grow feathers. They leave the nest. Then the mother starts building a new nest. She raises more chicks.

Fun Fact

After finches leave their nests, they join **flocks** with other young finches.

Life Cycle

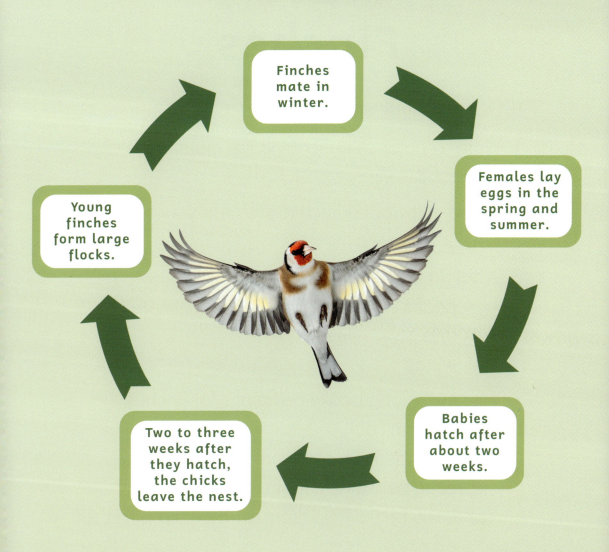

21

FOCUS ON
Finches

Write your answers on a separate piece of paper.

1. Write a sentence describing the main ideas of Chapter 3.

2. Would you want a finch to live near your home? Why or why not?

3. What do finches use to pick up food?
   - A. beaks
   - B. tails
   - C. wings

4. Why might long beaks be helpful for finches that eat from cacti?
   - A. Long beaks make them eat much less.
   - B. Long beaks help them avoid spikes.
   - C. Long beaks help them attack other birds.

Answer key on page 24.

Glossary

blend
To look the same as the other things in the area.

cacti
Plants that grow in deserts and often have spikes.

flocks
Groups of birds that live together.

grasslands
Large areas of land that are covered in grass and have few trees.

insects
Small animals with six legs.

ledges
Flat shelves of rock.

mate
To come together to make a baby.

perches
Things that birds can rest on.

To Learn More

BOOKS

London, Martha. *Robins*. Mendota Heights, MN: Focus Readers, 2021.

Murray, Julie. *Gouldian Finch*. Minneapolis: Abdo Publishing, 2023.

NOTE TO EDUCATORS

Visit **www.focusreaders.com** to find lesson plans, activities, links, and other resources related to this title.

Index

B
beak, 5, 9–10, 15

E
eggs, 19, 21

F
feathers, 7, 9, 11, 13, 15, 20

N
nest, 5, 7, 20–21

P
perches, 11

S
seeds, 5, 16

Answer Key: **1.** Answers will vary; **2.** Answers will vary; **3.** A; **4.** B